G. P. PUTNAM'S SONS • An imprint of Penguin Random House LLC, New York ⓟ Text copyright © 2020 by Irene Latham and Karim Shamsi-Basha • Illustrations copyright © 2020 by Yuko Shimizu • Penguin supports copyright. Copyright fuels creativity, encourages diverse voices, promotes free speech, and creates a vibrant culture. Thank you for buying an authorized edition of this book and for complying with copyright laws by not reproducing, scanning, or distributing any part of it in any form without permission. You are supporting writers and allowing Penguin to continue to publish books for every reader. • G. P. Putnam's Sons is a registered trademark of Penguin Random House LLC. • Visit us online at penguinrandomhouse.com • Library of Congress Cataloging-in-Publication Data is available. • Manufactured in China by RR Donnelley Asia Printing Solutions Ltd • ISBN 9781984813787
1 2 3 4 5 6 7 8 9 10 • Design by Eileen Savage • Text set in Maiola Pro •
The art for this book was first drawn with black ink on watercolor paper, then scanned in and colored using Adobe Photoshop.

Especially for Alaa, and for all the victims and survivors of the Syrian Civil War. —I.L.

I dedicate this book to my three children, Zade, Dury, and Demi,
and to all of those who do good. —K.S.-B.

For Tatiana Córdoba: without you this book would not have been completed. —Y.S.

The CAT MAN of ALEPPO

Irene Latham *and* Karim Shamsi-Basha

illustrated by Yuko Shimizu

putnam

G. P. PUTNAM'S SONS

مذكرة من علاء

عزيزي القارئ:

هذه قصة عن القطط وبني آدم في زمن الحرب، ولكن الأهم انها قصة عن الحب. لقد دفعني ولعي بالقطط الى انقاذ جميع انواع الحيوان قبل ان أهب لمساعدة أطفال و اهل سوريا، بلدي الحبيبة التي زعزعتها الحرب لمدة سبع سنوات. العديد من القلوب الرحيمة من كل أنحاء العالم مدت لي يد المساعدة لتحسين اوضاع المعوزين والمحتاجين هناك. بفضل كرم هؤلاء صار عندنا دار للأيتام و عيادات و ملاجئ للحيوانات السائبة التي تركها أهلها بسبب ظروف الحرب. يمكنكم أيضا مساعدتنا. معا نستطيع نجدة أطفال سوريا وخلق عالم أفضل للجميع

محمد علاء الجليل

A Note from Alaa

Dear Reader,

This is a story about cats and war and people. But most of all, it is a story about love.

Because of my love for cats, I'm now helping all kinds of animals, as well as people and children, orphaned from the war that gripped my country of Syria for seven long years. Generous people from everywhere are helping me support and improve my community. We now have an orphanage caring for many children, and clinics and shelters helping many animals.

You can help, too. Remember: both people and animals suffer pain, and all of them deserve compassion. Together we can make the world a better place!

—*Mohammad Alaa Aljaleel*

Alaa loves his city of Aleppo. He loves its narrow alleys and covered bazaars selling pistachios, jasmine soap, and green za'atar. He loves the boiled corn and dried figs offered on the street. Most of all, he loves the people of Aleppo. They are gentle, polite, and loving—like him.

Even when war comes to Aleppo, Alaa doesn't flee like so many others.

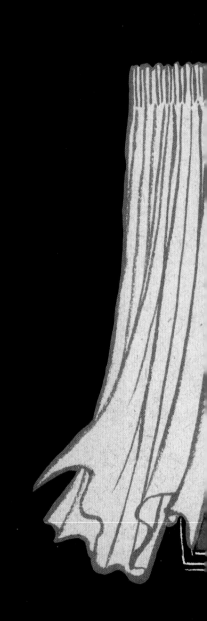

He continues his work as an ambulance driver.
He swerves through rubbled streets and carries the
wounded to safety. He comforts and holds them.
Alaa has a big heart.

Alaa's work is important, but he misses his loved ones. Where are they now? Are they safe?

He misses the way things used to be before the war. Aleppo's city center no longer echoes with the rich, exciting sounds of copper-pot pounding and traditional sword sharpening. His neighborhood is empty—

. . . except for the many cats left behind.

 The abandoned cats roam crumpled buildings and prowl filthy
alleyways for food. Their homes have been destroyed, and now no one
is left to love them and stroke their backs. No one is there to give them
food and water.

The cats' lonely, confused faces remind Alaa
of the loved ones he has lost. So many goodbyes!
So many people he hasn't been able to help. So
many days he feels lonely and confused, too.

On his way home from work, Alaa stops the ambulance. Two cats call to him from the branches of an ancient olive tree. Three more peek from a Syrian juniper tree. Alaa's big heart swells with love for them. Bombs may still fall, and his loved ones may never come back to Aleppo. But there is something he can do: he can look after the cats.

After his shift the next day, Alaa uses the little money he has to buy fresh meat.

When he unwraps the meat, the cats raise their heads and sniff the air. They are extra hungry.

"Taee, atta atta," Alaa calls. *Here, kitty kitty.* A dozen cats rush toward him, their tails high. He gives them bits of meat and talks softly to them. The cats chew and purr, purr and chew. Soon their bellies are full, and so is Alaa's heart. He smiles and pets the cats, and they love him back.

Alaa brings meat and water for the cats every day.
A dozen turns into twenty, and twenty turns into fifty.
He can no longer care for the cats alone. "I need a place
to keep them safe," Alaa tells his remaining neighbors.
"Together we can save them all."

Word spreads, and volunteers arrive. Donations pour in from many different countries. Everyone wants to help the cats of Aleppo.

Alaa collects enough money to buy a building with a shaded courtyard. He names the sanctuary the House of Cats Ernesto, in memory of a friend's beloved cat.

Soon cats are everywhere—orange cats, striped cats, white cats, gray cats, and black cats. For every cat, there's a dish of food and a bowl of water. Now when people must leave Aleppo, they bring their cats to Alaa before they go.

Hope and love fill people's hearts when they learn about the sanctuary's success, and they send more money. With so much support, Alaa is able to rescue other animals, too.

He builds a playground for the children still living in Aleppo.

He helps dig a well so everyone can have fresh water.
He distributes fruit, ma'amoul, and barazek cookies to
the people he meets.

Alaa's big heart is happy. All he did was love the cats, and that love multiplied and multiplied again. He still misses his loved ones and the way Aleppo used to be before the war. But now Alaa is known around the world as the Cat Man of Aleppo.

Alaa loves his city of Aleppo. He hopes one day soon its bazaars selling pistachios and jasmine soap will return, and he can enjoy eating boiled corn and dried figs. Meanwhile, he loves the sanctuary's courtyard filled with fat, sleepy-eyed cats. There's no place he'd rather be.

A Note from Irene

The moment I first learned of "the Cat Man of Aleppo" online in the fall of 2016, I knew I wanted to share this story. But I wasn't sure how—I am not from Syria, and my time in the Middle East was limited to the two and a half years during my childhood when our family lived in Riyadh, Saudi Arabia. It wasn't until early 2018, when I joined forces with Karim—a fellow Alabamian and striving children's book author, who emigrated from Syria—that this book really came to life. Thank you, Karim!

Here are the historical particulars: When the civil war in Syria reached the city of Aleppo in 2012, many families fled in order to save their own lives. Unfortunately, they were not able to bring their pets with them. This meant many cats became homeless. By October 2013, ambulance driver and paramedic Mohammad Alaa Aljaleel knew what he had to do—create a safe house for cats in his Masaken Hanano neighborhood. And that's exactly what he did.

When news broke of his efforts, he was joined by humanitarian Alessandra Abidin from Italy, and together they formed a Facebook page called *Il gattaro d'Aleppo* ("The Cat Man of Aleppo") and began collecting donations from around the world. They named the first shelter after Abidin's cat Ernesto, who had died of cancer.

As bombing continued in Aleppo, Alaa was forced to relocate the safe house several times. Currently the shelter is in the countryside west of Aleppo. To keep up with the latest news about the cats and other rescued animals, and for information about how to make a donation, follow Alaa on Twitter: @theAleppoCatman and on Facebook: @TheAleppoCatMen

Read more: http://syriadirect.org/news/a-crowd-sourced-animal-sanctuary-in-east-aleppo-teaches-compassion-'to-love-the-small-weak-cats-is-to-love-everything'/

—*Irene Latham*

A Note from Karim

My heart breaks for my country.

I grew up in Damascus and remember going to college in Aleppo in 1983, one of the most beautiful cities I had ever seen. Rich in history and culture, Aleppo harkens back to the early days of humanity, competing with Damascus for the title of Oldest Continuously Inhabited City on Earth. Unfortunately, the current war has destroyed many of Aleppo's historic treasures. It has also caused millions of people to become refugees, and thousands of animals to become homeless. Mohammad Alaa Aljaleel is doing his part by sheltering beings who cannot save themselves. I hope and pray that one day, Aleppo and Syria will be safe again for people and for animals. Until then, efforts like Alaa's will be hailed as heroic and noble.

Telling the story of the effects of war on people needs to be done, but on animals? They, too, suffer and caring for them illuminates what it means to be human. When Irene told me about Alaa and her desire to write a children's book, I jumped in to help. This led to a friendship I never could have anticipated—with the Cat Man himself! It has been my honor to speak numerous times with Alaa via phone and Facebook over the course of writing this book. His work now includes an orphanage for children left parentless from the war. We are grateful for his support and enthusiasm. His story is a tale we can all learn from, to hopefully become more compassionate human beings.

—*Karim Shamsi-Basha*

A Note from Yuko

As an illustrator, I am often asked where I find inspiration. In reality, my process is more about how much research I do rather than about inspiration. I have never been to Syria, but my task was to make the illustrations authentic.

I spent half of the nine months I had to complete this book solely on research—reading as many books as possible, viewing as many videos as I could find, and poring over photos. I also followed citizen journalists and photographers on Twitter (@AmeerAlhalbi, @alessioroa, @Delilsouleman, @SyriaCivilDef, @QZakarya, and @lirarain) who were on the ground, to fill in the gaps.

Alia Malek, whose memoir *The Home That Was Our Country* happened to be the first one I picked up, kindly suggested other books I should read, such as novels by acclaimed Syrian writer Khaled Khalifa. In addition to the list of references, I also read *My Country* by Kassem Eid and *Homes: A Refugee Story* by Abu Bakr al Rabeeah and Winnie Yeung. These books were powerfully moving and edifying. I am still reading, even now that the project is finished, because knowledge is power, and the learning does not stop when the project ends.

Outside of Alaa and some of the volunteers and kids who visit the sanctuary, most of the characters in the illustrations are composites of multiple Syrian people from reference photos I gathered. They are not "real" but also not "made up," as everything in each character, down to clothing, hairstyles, and accessories, are based on details provided in various reference photos. The setting was created in a similar way.

There have been two different cat sanctuaries, but in this book they are blended to give each illustration the right effect. Muhammad Mustafa and dina Amin, fellow artists from Egypt, helped me handwrite the Arabic correctly.

I fell in love with Aleppo and its people in the process. I hope to visit there one day.

—*Yuko Shimizu*

ART REFERENCES

Syrian Dust: Reporting from the Heart of the War by Francesca Borri, translated by Anne Milano Appel, Seven Stories Press, 2016.

Brothers of the Gun: A Memoir of the Syrian War by Marwan Hisham and Molly Crabapple, One World, 2018.

No Knives in the Kitchens of This City by Khaled Khalifa, translated by Leri Price, Hoopoe, 2016.

The Home That Was Our Country by Alia Malek, Bold Type Books, 2017.

We Crossed a Bridge and It Trembled: Voices from Syria by Wendy Pearlman, Custom House, 2017.

Escape from Aleppo by N. H. Senzai, Simon & Schuster, 2018.

Burning Country: Syrians in Revolution and War by Robin Yassin-Kassab and Leila Al-Shami, Pluto Press, 2016.

Last Men in Aleppo (film) directed by Feras Fayyad, 2017.